SandCastle™

Primeros Sonidos

I0878868

Gaby y Gastón

Cathy Camarena, M.Ed., and Gloria B. Ruff, M.Ed.

Consulting Editors

Lourdes Flores-Hanson, M.S.E., and Gloria Rosso-White

ABDO Publishing Company

capstone®

www.capstoneclassroom.com

Credits
Curriculum Coordinator: Nancy Tuminelly
Cover and Interior Design and Production: Mighty Media
Child Photography: Steven Wewerka, Wewerka Photography
Photo Credits: AbleStock, Brand X Pictures, Photodisc

ISBN 978-1-4966-0337-1 (paperback)

Printed in the United States of America.
874

SandCastle™ books are created by a professional team of educators, reading specialists, and content developers around five essential components that include phonemic awareness, phonics, vocabulary, text comprehension, and fluency. All books are written, reviewed, and leveled for guided and early intervention reading, and designed for use in shared, guided, and independent reading and writing activities to support a balanced approach to literacy instruction.

SandCastle Level: Beginning

Gg

ABCChDEFGH

IJKLLlMNÑOP

QRSTUVWXYZ

abcchdefgh

ijklllmnñop

qrstuvwxyz

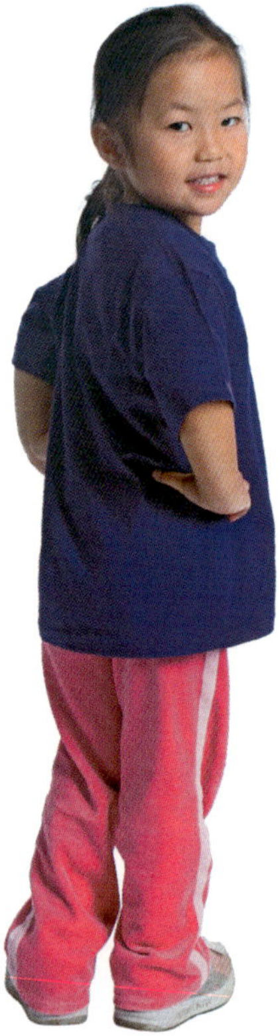

Gaby

Gastón

gato

ganso

gallina

globos

galleta

Este es un .

El  es blanco.

Mira la  .

Mira los  .

La  es redonda.

A Gaby le gustan los globos.

Ella tiene tres globos.

A Gastón le gusta
el gato.

El pelo del gato es
suave.

Al gato le gustan los globos.

Uno de los globos es azul.

¿Cuáles de estas cosas comienzan con **g**?

Más palabras que comienzan con g

gallo

garra

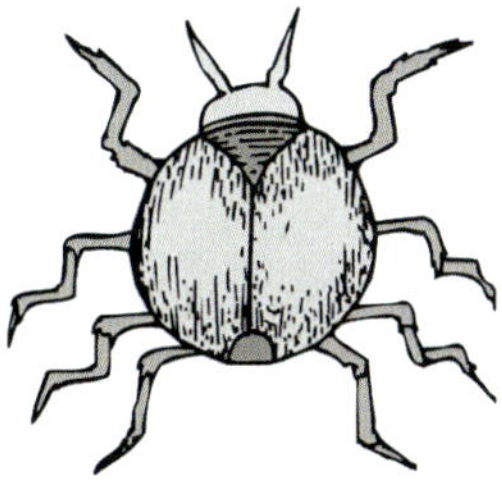

garrapata

gaviota

gorila

About SandCastle™

A professional team of educators, reading specialists, and content developers created the SandCastle™ series to support young readers as they develop reading skills and strategies and increase their general knowledge. The SandCastle™ series has four levels that correspond to early literacy development in young children. The levels are provided to help teachers and parents select the appropriate books for young readers.

Emerging Readers
(no flags)

Beginning Readers
(1 flag)

Transitional Readers
(2 flags)

Fluent Readers
(3 flags)

These levels are meant only as a guide. All levels are subject to change.

ABDO Publishing Company
www.abdopub.com

capstone®
www.capstoneclassroom.com